Getting to Philadelphia

Also by Thomas Devaney

You Are the Battery

Runaway Goat Cart

Calamity Jane

The Picture that Remains

A Series of Small Boxes

The American Pragmatist Fell in Love

Getting to Philadelphia
New and Selected Poems

Thomas Devaney

Hanging Loose Press
Brooklyn, New York

Published by Hanging Loose Press, 231 Wyckoff Street, Brooklyn, New York 11217-2208. All rights reserved. No part of this book may be reproduced without the publisher's written permission, except for brief quotations in reviews.

www.hangingloosepress.com

Printed in the United States of America
10 9 8 7 6 5 4 3 2 1

Hanging Loose Press thanks the Literature Program of the New York State Council on the Arts for a grant in support of the publication of this book.

Cover Art: Leroy Johnson, "Market - Frankford El," (2012)

Cover Design: Marie Carter

Photograph page 12: Zoe Strauss, "The El," (1986)

Photograph page 92: Will Brown, "Mr. Brown and Mr. Cannuccio," (1972)

ISBN 978-1-934909-57-7

Library of Congress cataloging-in-publication available on request.

for Francis Ryan

Contents

Preface *Getting to Philadelphia*

> Not long before I moved out of the Northeast, I met the poet Gil
> Ott, who asked me about my life, what I wanted to do. He told me a
> story about getting lost once in Northeast. "How does one get out of
> Northeast Philadelphia?" he asked. I ask, "Do you mean if you're in a car
> or bus, or do you mean like culturally?" "Both," he said.
> —"Northeast Spur," by Ryan Eckes, *General Motors* (Split Lip Press, 2018)

My ambition had always been to get out of Philadelphia. And I did. First, by way of a semester in Rome, and later by way of Brooklyn among a handful of writers, artists, and activists in the late 90s. Whenever I had to go back home I always felt sick to my stomach. I grew up in a part of the Northeast, a white ethnic working class enclave. The culture heavily policed itself. If you were in any way different, you paid a price. I know firsthand of at least seven suicides. Still, there were moments of miracles and wonder, which kept me alive then, and continue to feed me now.

History is what hurts, as the scattered life-moments are often in the in-between, on side streets, riding buses, days down along the river, all of the hidden spaces we create to survive. I'm most drawn to the untold stories, but I am equally compelled by those things, which cannot be told at all the interludes. Among other things, I carry the city's skyline in my heart.

Philadelphia is on the land of the Lenni-Lenape. If you know where to look, signs of the Lenape abound, in place names, and in the places themselves: Passyunk, Aarmingo, Kingsessing, Manayunk, Tioga, Wissahickon, Wissinoming. The name of the Lenni-Lenape itself has revealed something to me about the spirit of this place between two rivers. One translation of *Lenni* means real or genuine, and Lenape means person or the people. In short, the real people.

***

Philadelphia is a tough city and toughest on itself. For Sun Ra it was "Death's Headquarters." And W.C. Fields meant every mincing mean word when he said, "All things considered, I'd rather be in Philadelphia." He wanted that to be his epitaph. As the historian Ken Finkel wrote me, "So there's this theme running in the background (kind of like a flaw in the software or possibly even a virus) that Philadelphians can succeed – in theory. And this goes back to the 1680s. So it takes a creative individual like Lou Kahn (or John Moran, or others) to mine what the city is and come up with brilliance. But it's usually in the margins, not in the text."

Recalling Dr. J, the legendary 76ers player, one local sports writer hit upon a hard truth about this hard town: "Perhaps the ultimate tribute to Julius Erving is that no one recalls his ever being booed during his eleven seasons in Philadelphia." Sid Sachs, a curator and local historian, voices something of the city's confounding self-image: "I don't think it's a great city, but I don't think it's not."

Philadelphia happens to be one of the great cities of the world. It is the only U.S. city to have World Heritage status (no small thing). Concurrently, poverty is one of our most enduring problems. Philadelphia remains the poorest large city in the country. The momentous (historical and mythic) and the local (workaday) worlds coexist, but they rarely meet up. My grandmother Devaney boasted that she'd lived in Philadelphia her entire life, and had never seen the Liberty Bell!

***

One day I remember being jumped by four or five older teenagers who held me against a wall as one of them meticulously colored in my face with a permanent magic marker. The kind of permanent ink that makes you dizzy if you keep the cap off. They were punishing me, after having caught me writing on a school door. The main guy who beat me up and then blacked out my face was a graffiti writer named Floyd.

That summer my parents sent me to stay in Oley, Pennsylvania with family friends. It wasn't the country, but more working class rural. As far as I know, my parents didn't know about Floyd (or that horrific afternoon), but they knew enough to know I needed to get out of town. When I came back I heard Floyd had been missing. In early September, the maintenance crew found his body in the school furnace. He had fallen down into the chimneystack at Pollock. By all accounts it was ghastly. Questions lingered, did he go up there to get a tag, or to hide his drug stash? Was he alone? Nobody knows.

**

The first time I met the poet and small press publisher Gil Ott he asked if I had a sister. I said, *Ahh*, do you know Colleen? (see poem "Things We String Together.") He said, no, "I know a woman named Maureen Devaney." *Oh*, that's my mother (and he pronounced the last name right too, the softer sounding *De-vann-ee*, not the harder sounding *De-vain-ee*). Gil brightened, "Well, Maureen is the real thing. A great advocate for people with disabilities." Gil also was, and she still is. He worked for an organization called Liberty Resources (a name I absolutely love). Equally great, my mom's nonprofit is called Vision for Equality.

Before he died, I saw Gil. He looked gray, but Gil had always looked gray. Now he seemed like an ashened character from one of his stories—one right out of Poe, Lippard, or Kafka—if Kafka was from at K&A, Kensington and Allegheny.

Here is Gil as an apparition afoot on the city streets: "I don't know you and I don't like you... Why have you come? Who have you come to meet? Here are two columns of people, one to the left and one to the right, regularly spaced. A gauntlet. Avert your eyes. They don't see you. Everyone has his own problems and hopes. You could be out of here in the blink of an eye if you'd move a little faster. Keep walking. Every step your feet sink deeper into the ground." From the story "The City" in Ott's Singing Horse Press title *PACT*.

My own poems are not ghost stories, but they are filled with ghosts.

It is strange that I never consciously set out to write about Philadelphia. Except for some of the more recent pieces, it was never a deliberate factor. Now I realize it's been there all along, a prevalent source. A sound I know in my bones. One I have been marked by, and one which in turn I have marked. My own take on why any poem needs to be is the music that it makes must be something more than merely a transcription of its own tongue. The *getting* part has to be the continual approach as much as it is anything else.

trying to live as if it were morning

Where in the great glare was I

Under the sun I saw two kids along a long fence
walking   and then fast to a cut, and then we all
were gone. I saw an empty delivery truck with its back
opened as it sped away, twice in the same day.
There was a side field under the sun and I could see
that the grass was wet and dense, with some night still in it.
It had to be freshly cut, but there were no mowers or municipal
ground crews anywhere. A field in my nose,   and even now
not a soul to share it.   On the edge of Chinatown an older
couple had just found a bench. They sat closely and looked
straight ahead, one or the other patted the top of the other's hand.
          I saw that the secret source of light appeared from a brick
pavement stained white at the edges. I saw a splash of little suns
scatter and then re-station themselves in the air, light speaking
to light in the eyes of a pair of sunglasses.

A Week in the Childhood of W.C. Fields

W.C. Fields played in the cider fields of Tioga. Back
then no one ever said Philadelphia or Darby, and
buffeting was a trade. Steel tongs and ice wagons,
as a child Fields had a sooty face and was always out
playing, or "in the game," as he'd say. One was
juggling, and the other they liked to call "Never Give
a Sucker an Even Break." Monday was a milk cart.
Tuesday, an open-body dump truck and a gang of
cursing boots. Wednesday was a boxcar that everyone
said carried raw sugar, and everyone had the sugar to
prove it. Thursday was a visit from two dicks in sweaty
suits. Friday afternoon: cigarettes and a mess of money
out on the street. Saturday day was haircuts for the men,
John the Barber, and the day numbers; the whole day
was a half-day and bucket of bleach. And Saturday night
was a whole other day: thieves and mothers sharpening
their knives, girls with curls and bald men. And always
the singing and the fighting—the police could do nothing.
Sunday was another country: a bath, a window, the ring
of the red trim wash basin, and looking at a picture
of the old Dutch settlement. The drawing was too small
to be this neighborhood, but in a sober moment, his father
told him that it was, back before any of them were born.

Trying to live as if it were morning

Every character in Dostoevsky is going to be in the hospital
       after this poem.
The underground man with a baseball bat, clearing house
"Philly-Style," and from what I've seen
       it would be true.

I put the Brothers K and their endless array of calamities
       out with my pinky.

I don't go in for the ping-pong of rational-irrational,
       possible-impossible—
The sad, lucid, mad, attractive, murky
       and yes, horrible overcoat of Paradox, Pennsylvania.

I don't need that.

The Bros. K are gone.
The problem of fake hamburger or even real hamburger remains.

The Past at my back,
Back in the past, I agree with John Coltrane
       when he says, "War begets war."

I drive all around my neighborhood with "the Idiot"
       in the front basket of my bike.
When he falls out we pick him up and keep going.
He's clever in a way that *any* other person might be killed for.

Of course, people don't fuck with us.

It's the old game of imposing order where there isn't any
       then calling yourself on it.

The ancients called it gravity; the modernists job security.
The people after lost a lot of weight and went home pissed off
Not believing they were home when they actually were,
          so they never really slept.

It's the kind of trouble a fleet of blimps "up in flames"
Might cause flying over an Olympic stadium as seen
          on a video loop—
                    but really real anyway, like on fire.

People point out the violence I do to my own words,
How uncareful I can be—I duck under their commentary.
My copy of *Crime and Punishment* is under the aloe plant
          all buckled and stained from water.

A man I respect said there hasn't been any "breakthrough work"
          since sometime in the 1930's.
Sometimes for me it would just be breaking things.
Like my uncle's a "good guy," but
The precinct Captain pulled his back-up.
He shouldn't be here. We don't talk about it.

Take out a piece of paper and write down:
Man the builder, Man the destroyer, Man the eater
          of donuts, butter cake, and pork buns.

The experimenter said he, or some recombinant
He and She "unsettles all things."
Even though that's cool, I don't unsettle "all things."
I don't have enough time.
There's enough nonsense without that nonsense.

I'm not here to settle that.
I'm here to write a poem because I'm a morning person
          and it's morning.

This is a morning poem.

They're fighting in Atlantic City, in Atlantic City

The urge to put question marks after everything.
Counting the loss, magnetically stripped:
    1-800 generally desensitized.
Now that I'm saying this keeping it going isn't proof.
They're fighting in Atlantic City, in Atlantic City.
Legs on a chair, three fingers resting lightly on her shin.
You don't have to get abstract to see everyone's beat-up badly.
It's not the future, it's Lunchtime all around.
The many ways you think about shaking off the outfit.
The kindergarten teacher's countdown to silence.
This quiet, this time of day — call it a nap.
The fried salmon burger and the salad were good.
Where did we leave the exclamation points?
The G train took me home in twenty minutes, I was grateful.
I don't live anywhere.

Deliberate for Lorenzo Thomas

In the basement of Double Happiness
there's no sitting on your secrets,
and that's the room's dark truth.
The man nearby doesn't nod,
but opens his marked and watery eyes wider.
I take it as hello, and it is.
His eyes are older than he is
and he is not so young.
It's how he looks when he looks,
and looks good too.
Sharp and serious, one of the older guys
you say hello to, but can never know,
and yet know all the same.
Smoke in the spotlight, and so we talk.
He isn't from Philadelphia,
          "A good place to be *from*," he says.
We sit for another New York minute, and
another one, and I'm still there now.
More smoke slowly works its way from
one end of the room to the other.

Getting to Philadelphia

It's late November when you depart – Thanksgiving.
Hit a hard snag at 34th street, and for two blocks and thirty minutes
       aren't going anywhere.
Two million people wave to NBC cameras in front of Macy's,
you wave too into an ocean of police officers, TV crews
and two million people like yourself, except that
they aren't going to Philadelphia – you wade through
the understandable urge to kill a man,
or a few dozen kids or a half a dozen cops, and see one huge barge (floating)
with HOLLYWOOD, Statue of Liberty, London Bridge, and on top
a big piano–and the man waving, you guess, is John Tesh, the alien.

Somehow at Penn Station you get tickets
and somehow, a glazed donut and a small coffee,
somehow, a seat on NJ Local to Trenton.
The man sitting next to you lives in Yardley, PA.
You quiz him on the parade and the wind and the HOLLYWOOD float.
He confirms the John Tesh sighting.
He turns away, and you out the window
to late Autumn's Big Brown suitcase sale,
looking gorgeous on Jersey's pared down brown back.
Like Kmart had a sale on every shade brown paint
and your grandfather decided to putt around the backyard,
paint brush hanging from his back pocket.
The short tan coat of a sleeping hill,
cement cold browns proud in light,
empty billboard advertising a flash flood of triple whirlpools.
Brown birds on a brown-red ridge, and what someone said
about "the ominous mud," makes sense in the flight of window,
and a pile of railroad ties, pick-up-stick style,
everything in a ditch, and the only tree with all its leaves
casts a shadow all wrong for the light on dried-out grass, further

back, the still point of a lumber yard turns into another stand
of trees emptying into a side pool of muddy water.

And the wind, the wind's funneling leaves all around the train and
its eager for you to know where it came from. For some reason
when you reach Trenton it looks like the police are waiting for you,
but today you're lucky, since the skeleton shift doesn't make the time,
so you get quick to the SEPTA local.

Then inside, the SEPTA poster, We're Getting There.
Then the bridge, the neon glow against the all grey sky
    TRENTON MAKES WORLD TAKES

Finally, Aunt Sharon's for dinner. Everyone there
and you say hello
and you say you were at the parade
and they ask, touching your arm, if you're all right
because you're told and will see footage
one of those gigantic balloons, Cat in the Hat, got loose
injuring up to at least four people, and your glasses steam
        in the mash-potato kitchen.

1997

The Sky Under Construction

Sweet Jesus crashes to the sidewalk.

Part of the building has just slipped off—

and everyone is stopped in an instant circle

around the ledge.   The city performs a pause

and miraculous someone says no one was killed.

We are huddling outside of Dazzling Nails.

Even before the scene is taped off it was taped off.

The slab cracked in two, a smooth phantom dolphin,

and the crowd extending down the street.

Closer in, a group of men look with an eye to see

how the ledge might be moved. But there's another lift

of the eyes, up to the building and vacancy

where the ledge had been. The hole there, an homage

to stone that has lived so long in the sky,

and the ambition to build into the brilliance,

a turning wheel.   I heard a Berlioz song

mingling with a spin class, five or six stories up:

the windows wide open in a clear yet distant throttle—

Does anyone really know where music comes from?

Wilderness of blue and glass: the sky perfectly adrift,

perfectly clear, a blazing stream of duststrewn daylight,

its *spin*, nothing out of place.

The Blue Stoop

Who remembers the blue stoop?
I am laughing at the question—Who?
Everybody. All the names.
Like an early book of the Bible,
it isn't just names, they go deep
and make three wide steps, three
very wide steps, an everywhere.
There is Franny and Kim.
Amy, Gary, and George. Dawn Ann
and her redheaded brother Bobby.
BA, Matthew, Paula, and Rob.
Tommy Fliss and all the Flisses.
Goddamn Steve Fliss. Steve smoking Fliss.
Anthony's mother is leaning out the window.
Does she ever go out? Yes, every day.
She leans out the window all day long.
Anthony's uncle played the trumpet.
Everybody knows that, but when we say
        he played the trumpet
we mean he played with everybody.
Yes, Tony Bennett, but have you ever heard
of Al Martino? Guy Lombardo? People,
big bands—he played with them all, and
in some third-floor heaven he still is.
People say, *Once upon a time a call was a dime.*
They say more than I can say here, they're living.
They say, *Don't forget where you're from,*
but I don't have to, I never left.
Recently somebody said the blue stoop looks smaller
        than it used to.
I guess they know what they're talking about,
but don't tell that to Michael, Michael, and Michael,

and a generation of Roses weaned on a fresh coat
of swimming pool paint every few years.
All the dirty kid faces that will never be clean.
Those are my faces.

Brilliant Corners

The magic parts before they were burned up and vacuumed.

A sound so light as if no one was there at all.

Your body a buffer between *the same word said at the same time* and other hyper jinx chances.

The dustup made the light look more grey than green.

Time was opened up wider then, so wide in fact that even now it isn't all the way shut.

Horns, sirens, acoustic panels: plenty of *three people can keep a secret, if two are dead* stories to go around.

A late and great string quartet playing in the next room.

I couldn't tell where the music was coming from, and I didn't care.

I was back in high school practicing a clarinet concerto.

And for months, upended by the harp on the headphones in the Chopin waltz.

Walkman freewheeling Sony Walkman—

And only one other person in the world.
                                        It does not matter where we fell in, we did.

What she called AC/DC I called AC/DC. Though Monk wasn't Monk, he was MONK: avuncular, like an uncle with no glass in his glasses, poking his fingers *in* to show us.

Not silence, but the stillness of the world; and yet even being still didn't mean you couldn't scratch your nose.

How you once heard the sound of water running under a heavy manhole cover. The Great Spirit echoing in the old city pipes; a ghost river running under Allegheny Avenue.

Not sound, but the fact of sound.

Not sound or the fact of sound, but the fact of sound after the sound was gone.

HOW WILL I FIND YOU?

I AM WEARING A RED HAT SHE SAID.

I SAID OK—I'LL LOOK FOR YOU.

EACH RED HAT I SAW I SAW YOU.

THOSE HATS STOPPED ME.

AND MORE RED HATS.

YOU TEXTED I'M LATE.

YOU TEXTED I'M HERE NOW.

IT WAS WET, BUT NOT RAINING.

I AM HERE, *I'M HERE* YOU SAID.

STILL I COULDN'T SEE YOU.

A MAN TOLD ME TO GET A JOB, YOU SAID.

AND WHAT DID YOU SAY?

JOBS COME AND GO BUT I HAVE SOMETHING ELSE TO DO:

THE WORK WE ARE IN.

IT IS GREAT AND IT IS REAL.

BUT IS IT ENOUGH?

YES IT IS.

AND NO, IT IS NOT.

ENOUGH, ENOUGH.

YES, ENOUGH.

AND THEN ENOUGH, ENOUGH

ENOUGH, ENOUGH.

COMING DOWN THE STREET.

OREGON AVE

You can't find a place to smoke anymore
Ro says, smoking and rifling
through her handbag looking for a number.
She sits in the backseat with Meg.
They're not singing.
The ballgame's on inside and outside
the game is always on.
Actually, sometimes they do sing.
What year is the car, a '98?
A Ford? A Focus? They always tip too.

There is dust, always; and terrible dirt;
but if that's what you see you're hardly looking.
We believe in the front stoop.
We believe in banging pots and pans and honking horns.
We believe that in the heat of day shadows come back.
The trashcan on fire says *things are hotting up*.
The street's a mix, water, water ice, LIVE CRABS,
jumbo jets, firecrackers.
Summer days are huge and often overlap late into fall.
Seriously, when you have a good spot, why move the car.

The Legend of Cornbread

The history of graffiti begins with Cornbread (check the dates).

Scaling the wall at the Zoo, he wrote on the back thigh of an elephant.

At International Airport, he sidestepped security to write on the side of the Jackson Five's jet plane: CORNBREAD LIVES!

Big C and a Double-Bubble B. Straight-ahead never meant straight:—it's a style.

I remember most the piece between the Schuylkill Expressway and 30th Street Station. A very tall, long-lettered piece. Who knows, a self-portrait? How the flat red-fade and the dusty Krylon yellow disappear into each other.

Younger, Cornbread wanted to get out of the neighborhood.

He rode the Subway and the bus routes, and then the Frankford El. His ambition grew.

He owned North Philly. He eclipsed SEPTA and went ALL-CITY. To Fern Rock all the way out to Point Breeze, Hunting Park and all over Olney Ave.

King of the parking lots in Overbrook Park.

Moving, he built alliances, branching out and over—and up again.

And again, at night and young in Juniata, Oxford Circle, Wissinoming, and East Germantown.

There was talk—and it was more than just talk—warning-signs and threats aplenty. Undercover cops, gang members, good neighborhoods, and always other rival writers *X-ing* him out.

Make a list: he crossed *the never step your foot into Devil's Pocket*, because of the Irish, and wrote. Hopped the fence at the *don't cross 10th Street*, because of the Italians, for the bread trucks; and he hit-up at the cross-streets of all *don't even think about it* cross-streets, 8th and Butler.

Longing, reaching, walking—and telegraphing his walk – down the street, down the way, all around. Bashed. Cut. Ratted-out and Jailed.

The old guys ribbed him hard, "Travel much in Concord?"

Yet, he went at liberty.

For me, it isn't if Cornbread was a hero not. He was a giant. A giant in a land of giants.

The Home Book

Notes from a notebook summer 2018

I killed a big fly with your book.

*

Sid says everything gets stored in New Jersey.

*

The Quaker City, City of Brotherly Love, home of the Lenni-Lenape, City of Neighborhoods, Bicentennial City, Death's Headquarters, the Hidden City.

Not only a city of hard-luck and History, but how the heart and the fist beat together as echoing impulses.

*

The heart is not a disembodied thing, it has to have an anatomy that runs into the neighborhood.—Jane Jacobs.

*

Franny at huge block party at Harrowgate Park, at Tioga and Jasper, and earlier on O Street at Piccoli Playground.

*

Rick telling me more about Harry G. Ochs Jr. in the Market at his Prime Meats stall. Ochs wasn't his name at all, he was an Italian, not German. Rick slips back into the clatter, a receding series of *See yiz later, See yiz later.* And to an actual friend, over his shoulder: *To hell with you Jack. To hell with youse all.* Check, check, check—that tone, that tone.

*

My summer of sleepwalking and vow to name the ghosts.

*

June 16: The reality is next week the doors will be closed. What's the question again?

—*Curator at the Philadelphia History Museum*

*

The double *cluck-cluck* of the Frankford El in my skull with the triple *cluck-cluck-cluck* of the Broad Street Subway.

*

Remembering a lunch cart at 19th and the Parkway. The guy ahead of me says, "Alright Cornbread, see you tomorrow." And there I am, *next*. Place my order and work-up the courage, and, finally: "Are you Cornbread?" "Yes I am," he almost smiles. "That's me," he says. "Cornbread the writer?" "Hell no," Cornbread laughs, "That's the North Philly Cornbread. I'm the West Philly Cornbread!"

*

The *lub*-dub, *lub*-dub of the floor-to-ceiling heart at the Franklin Institute, on a grade school field trip.

*

July 18: Turn off Broad in a car with Ken onto Belfield Ave around 4:30 pm. The purple façade of a ramshackled bar catches our eyes on the south west side of the street. We pull over. The outline of the sign for *Sparky's CLUBHOUSE* in the shape of a house. A pretty good plume of smoke puffing-out of the sign's chimney stack. Also, half of the back roof is missing. It's more than a wreck. A long story, but almost by accident, the man at the auto repair shop next door tells us that the owner's sitting in her car across the street. Beyond believing, she is there. Car door half-open, she's listening to the radio. We cross over and she's happy to talk. Her name is Jean Wilson. Ms. Wilson speaks with an inflected French accent, almost Creole: "I've been in the States since '61. I work a tailor shop for 10 years. I work at the restaurant for 10 years. Then I've been at the bar here for 30 years." Ms. Wilson sits in her car with her back to the bar.

*

Too hot, too soon, another *feels hotter than 100 day*. Early early morning at the bus stop, feels like I am breathing-up the last bit of air of the day. Neck already a little wet, and *like that* an Asali Solomon story is in my head: "No one gets too comfortable at the bus stop on Forty-eight and Spruce. A tree or two shades the iron bench in summer, but nothing can keep out the wet-cotton humidity on a day like today, even this early. The gray sidewalk is hot, the asphalt is hotter, and the playground behind the bus stop is empty. It is eight o'clock, and Rufus is running late for work."—from "First Summer" in *Get Down*.

*

On phone with Zoe at night, Muriel Rukeyser and a hundred other things come up. "It's a long story," she says, "All of these things are. The Gulf War through now: if Vets are saying *what the fuck*, then what the fuck?"

*

Run into John the Barber at the Reading Terminal. John had a place on 8th St. near Catharine. He cut my hair over 27 years ago, but still doesn't miss a beat, "Hey, buddy!" I say my name, and John says, "Yeah, yeah Tommy baby."

Back home go looking for a Kevin Varrone poem. It's from *the philadelphia improvements* book:

clarion

he cuts hair in his basement now. he lives in a rowhouse
in which he was born. when he was fifty-two his mother died.
he got married. they have no children. he & his wife
like going on cruises but he has diabetes. I eat a lot of fish he says,
joe. I don't correct him. he puts on the hi-fi. standards.
he has a drum kit next to his barber chair. he plays,
not with sticks but brushes. it sounds like falling
asleep. a bottle of sea breeze skin tonic.
a calendar from new noodle heaven.
I ask were noodles & that other guy that swears & limps
will hang out now. shhh shhh shhh say the drums.
stay still he says. I close my eyes. the scissors are seagulls.

Kevin's books are crammed next to Pattie McCarthy's. Some of Pattie's
books are pulled out. I thumb through looking for her "philadelphia :
predella." By steps, I find it, predella in *Table Alphabetical of Hard Words*:

passyunk triangle— who can resist big band
renditions of traditional carols? who can
resist commemorative tea kettles & liberty
bell ornaments ? not I. who can resist
such festivity ? not I, not
even I. the weather a wintery 4:00 p.m.
all day (like buffalo) & the sky so low
it gives me a stomachache.
it's a multi-river city, but I can't
see a river from here
in the morning you
nod without speaking—
afraid of losing your metaphysics.
as long as I'm working on poems
I don't have to grade papers— who
can resist a meander off

the grid, the missed
opportunities of a triangle ?

the picture that remains

Algon Avenue

The store has been shuttered
for a few years now,
though I keep coming back to stand
at the window.

The bricks are as poignant
and stubborn as the men
who put them there.
As stubborn as a blood feud
that lives on into another confusion.
And there is nothing confusing about that.
The same men tell me
to just *move along.*
What does it have to do with you?

Even Algon Ave. was abbreviated;
a mason's chip off
of Algonquin.

But the day pushes on
to this pavement and glass:
handprints and feet, paw prints
in the cement.
The avenue won't go away.
        This spot,
the stippled sedge grass,
a forgotten photograph
in a book.
        There's a fascination
exerted
by the dented statement
of the shade;
the grate
and its interlocking triangles.

Mr. Uska and his Dog, 1973

A dirt street followed me here,
Mr. Uska said. Still breathing, yes,
I can shoe your horse
and beat and make
just about anything with steel.
       When I work I trust my hands;
when you know your tools
you don't need the light, whereas
when you have a good dog
you don't need a clock.
When she was a puppy
she liked the sun too much.
Back then everything was a disguise:
the forge was a dark woods; a hammer
in the air was the end of the world, and
the end of that was the 4th of July.
No, it's really the sun that makes it dark.

The Uskas, Mr. Uska said, were hard workers,
but we kept to ourselves.
No one ever knew how to say my name
and I didn't correct them.

The Picture that Remains

Buzzing in the glass,
the soda water has gone to my head.

Sitting at the counter, looking
back out the door, the street's
vacancy is demanding:
STOP. LOOK
  AT YOUR SHOES.
  REPAIR THEM NOW.
I continue to look: the green
on a dark green plywood sheet
where the window used to be.
Someone's second best suit.
A Buick Special that clicks, starts, and goes.
The Shoe Man's silhouette, a sign itself.
The storefront window of The Wire Works.
The cross Old Timer will have none of it.
Of what?
        The oldest old mean guy
who stops by the luncheonette every day
and says "Clear as a comb,"
and "In living memory of the James A. Garfield
        Administration."

Across the street, the street noises
no longer entered the room.

The doorframe has been stripped down
but there's another layer in its place—
worn hash marks,
thick paint-brushed staples;
and what good is the silence?

It doesn't even hold up the windowpanes.
Nothing can. It can crack
or crash any minute.

In the front window sill two cats scrunch
into the last patch of sunlight.

The largest of the pictures was deinstalled.
The crew carried it away,
and this is the one that remains.

Saturday Night Special

The headlights were on
a pure swear.
And all these years now
you are still swearing,
even with the music off.
Like that
the '64 Caddie—
nothing like it.
A half inch closer,
       they kept on saying.
Accidents
enter backwards,
their past always
before them.
Jackknife
on the off ramp; a fork
inside a fork;
a horn and the street
lights; the sound
that should be a sound,
but is without any volume,
or place to go: incidents,
investigations.
And so we stare and stare.

THE BEST STYLES

The window said
"THE BEST STYLES
ARE ON DISPLAY INSIDE."
But the window was loaded
with Men's dress shoes,
and this was many years ago,
and the store and shoes are gone,
and that is a matter of fact.
There are mirrors
and plate-glass windows—
the noon-time sun piling on
forgetful glass, but here
and there some of those shoes
are still around in their galoshes,
and in a bank of clouds
that follow them around.

Don Cook's Brother's Cadillac

There's a story there, god knows
there is. But good luck in finding it.

That Old Block

Worst things happened on that block.
Everyone knows and nobody does.
Even back then it was far away;
Even to the blocks not far off,
It was another world. It always was.
Those doors nailed shut,
Those out of date blinds,
Piles of evil boxes.
All those things that have no backside.
A period of dirt and rumor has set in.

Rear Window

The collapse of tenderness
and no place to park.
But there was an open spot.
Shift and reverse—
the vantage
of the rear window, eyes
over the shoulder.
A need and skill met in
a semi-blind act.

All that happened—
all that needed to happen.

Shall we simply sit here and stare?

Whichever year it was,
the make of the car
ten or twelve years
older than that.
All of those years
in one: The one of the auto.
The one of the war.
The one of which side
        of the street
                did we park?

After the last argument,

the last silence
        of the last two people
                to hear it.

Together, that's the light we are in.

The Thing I Must Tell You

after a recording of Wisława Szymborska

Like a stone thrown straight into the river.
The eyes, the face and eyes. The urgency
to see the only eyes that those eyes must see.

They're hazel and do not flinch.
They say: *Yes, Right,* or *No.*
They're licked. Or:
Like running across the Boulevard,
hand holding an arm, or another hand,
tomorrow
       and now.
Rye bread, vodka, and a canvas bag.
           Late in the day,
everyone's favorite Aunt Peg cuts to the quick
in Port Richman; and Jimmy "the Mayor"
Lemanowicz WILL BE BACK TOMORROW,
or so says a sign on the river wards.
A lip of light on the head shining ahead.
It's never not late. And again:
Jak kamień rzucony do wody.
It's me or not me I overheard the Baba say
       to her Alan, Alan.
Held, not in a gentleness,
       but in the pitch black quiet of her coat.
There, there was nobody else. No horde in that space
that could push us out.

Sessler's or Hibberd's Bookstore?

I am guessing the name still. I'm conflating them.
The ceiling high and dark in the daylight.
That bookstore on Walnut below Broad,
on the sleepy, rundown side of Broad.
Its front window was very large and very dusty.
No bag-check. Not so much talking. And no questions
        asked. Stage whispers and footsteps, deep back
into the stacks and all the way up to the ceiling.
A 19th century wrought-iron gate separates the front of
the store from rows of leather-bound books, maps, folios,
discrete erotica, and a sumptuous wall of Charles Dickens.

A friend emails me to say Hibberd's new and used books
was next door to Sessler's rare books.
        And be sure to look-up Mable Zahn (1890-1975).
She began work at 15, took over when the owner died.
Ms. Zahn remains a giant in color plated books, Audubon,
        and other treasures.
Until the last day the store was opened, the staff kept her
reading glasses up at the register.
        How many books do I have from Hibberd's?
I have no idea. I want to lie and say *every last one*, but
I can say that my *Autobiography of Alice B. Toklas* t-shirt
still surfaces every time I move.

philly makes philly breaks

Raccoon

I didn't know the strength of
         a city raccoon, which busted out through
my chest, escaped down the side street.
Wild eyes of the raccoon's lightning,
lighting up reflectors
from here to Water Street.
A raccoon uses the full weight of its body
to get what it wants.   Something
in me, some immediate want.
Unburdened by one weight, lit
by another.   Cravings
in the headlights.   On the night
in question, I was a wretch along
railroad tracks, a bulky brown sofa dumped
without its cushions.
Christ and a mouth-thirst,
               all my Jersey devils.

With every trashcan lid it flips off
         the raccoon feels more itself.
Prophets and raccoons share
a single ritual: they wash their food.
The row homes sleeping.
The row homes counting their bricks.
            Every night raccoons follow
the same path, they don't go far.
Cellophane wrappers coil in the crabgrass,
dogs down by the river, trails of cinders, piles of
gravel, lines not marked but closely kept.
            Reflectors everywhere: sneakers,
bicycle parts, a STOP sign in a pile of junk in
someone's shared alley space; and rows of painted poles
in the vibrant dark.   Poles of concrete sunk
into the sidewalks so no one can park there.

Permission to be Crushed

Why I had to leave.

Why I had to walk down certain streets so as not to walk down others.

As soon as you know, you know.

To battle the daemons of my enclave who

give permission every time to smash bottles

against the sewer wall until the feeling passes, or

you run out of Michelobs.

Wide awake in a recent dream, I cannot scale the brick wall.

I can't go over it, and can't go through. I could draw a map,

 or make a plan, but why?   That wall is not my wall anymore.

In another dream the next night, a rooting pain

in my right heel.

Extract a vine from the old planter's wart.

It's a muscled vein-root that I can only keep a hold on

with great difficulty, and only with both hands.

Over two feet long, fighting as if to get away;

After, I rub and rub the heel with my thumb.

It's been there all along.

Draw a map, make a plan, whatever you want to call it.

It's taken years to figure out, there's no figuring it out.

Ear Tool

Fuck the right fit.
On a ladder
my head hot
near the ceiling
light,
all that working
class crap.
Can hear
the guys
on the jobsite
next door.
The whole
thing
about
the whole
thing, *that*
whole
elbow
brush elbow,
half a nod
short
OK
thing.

Background Noise

Children have their own music; and the owls.
The Snow Owl: always five blinks off the beat.
A friend pointing to the eaves at the wildlife preserve:
"This guy's a menace. Barker from a bad circus."
Shake hands with your sister Kate, shake feet with the owls.
City kid, bet your life I was afraid of the owl.
Yes, if you won't bet: still afraid of the owls.

Hour of bottles and breaking glass, not yet day.
Growl of truck, tucked back in, hard to say when
You stopped hearing it. On this particular, Morning says,
The day runs behind the day. Not a dreamsong,
It's true, waiting for Mary. Mary Mary,
      Why all the trucks backing up?
Softly and low-toned. Emulation and the owl.

Books on bookcase are taking single breaths.
They want *out*. Like X used to say, such and such
Was under wraps. Honestly, one reason you felt at home
Was you didn't have to keep an eye on your stuff.
Shaped by a half-dozen voices, sighs, cries: hear
Tom. Thomas. Tommy Wheels.

Memory Corkscrews So You Can't Remember It

I make my prayers in another part of the city,
but they keep blowing back:
   Philly makes, Philly breaks—
What the hell are you looking at?
At the end of the year something
called Sneaker Day,
Swedish Fish and tail pipes in the breeze.
Two kids jamming 2,000-plus Styrofoam cups into
a chain-link fence, spelling-out R U N right along
the spillway.

Too young to drive, but opinions carried weight.
The first day of the Cadillac, that first week,
the whole summer, brilliant sunbeads after the rain:
the two-toned Charcoal Caddie.
Jerry Vale came in to get his haircut.

And did they still wear the ponytail style?

Eventually there was a car, a hobbled '74 Pinto,
cheap and easy to park. Driving circles
around one another,
   you can run yourself over.
Eating lunch, C said she wouldn't say things
like that, but she wasn't telling me not to,
but maybe don't. I had pizza and a lemonade.

All rumors reset in a blaze over Jersey.

Did the Night Shift and Day Shift ever speak
to each other again?

The year without talking, but music
coming from the little blue car booming inside out—
all the livelong day; a pulse as much as a sound.
        There would be no outside then.
Even the river ran more quietly, the FM radio
streaming more smoothly over the stream.

You almost had to get your ear wet to hear it.

River Song

Return back over the river, driving
through New Jersey is like a hand-held film,
the camera is shaky and everything hits you too fast.
Humming and the sod farm,
                                    for you it was a moor.
Spirit says, *float* and *pile on the truck bed*.
Spirit says, *the fire in the glove box is a catastrophe*
that will never die, as long as we continue to die and die.
From 20-gallon trashcans with swinging lids to sandy soil
– and to the middle school grounds and back.

You laugh though never crack a smile.
Your sister is somewhere in the state:
Bridgeport, Cross Keys, Jutland, Bayonne?
We reach a point where you are singing.
This is your CD playing, you singing
over your own song, over you, to you.

Morning in Runnemede

Not house music, but the house shaking,
and the roof on fire too.
The neighborhood dogs howling with the sirens,
and all other high frequencies.
And everyone else just mad.

I chart the baseball and soccer seasons
from another field. Motorcyclists on riverfront.
"Two Tickets to Paradise," across parking lot.
Decade of the Corner Deli. June's coming fast.
Tell whatever story you want, all I know
          is my dad said hustle.
Ambition meant something else altogether.
One thousand wrong answers, what I knew.

A gift economy would have been nice.
But even now I'd take a single sentence
that swings, something
          in the pocket,
                    verve for,
                    nerve from,
what things may come.
          And Jack and Jackie too,
just broken-up
enough, alack, no kind act
          to go unpublished.

Grandmother said, "Watch out."
Are quotes necessary?
Not really, and she never could have said
all I have her saying; though she did
have one refrain I loved—"Don't get old."
That was it, and *out of the house now.*

String of strip malls, strip clubs,
        Roger Wilco discount liquor stores, diners—
New Jersey a whole lot more than its tropes
and its starched-white State Troopers.
We swept into teams:
the Uniforms vs. the Uniforms.
Some new glitch-hitter foaming
        outside the fence.
Forget Second Base. Forget the Outfield,
        or even the Bench.
How about the trumpet or a clarinet?
The marching band queers.
Save my fucking life. "Boys Don't Cry,"
unless with all your heart
and a heady sense of what to wear.
No succor for the soccer suckers;
though I had a pair of black MITERS.
And Village Thrift so frikkin cheap.
Camden Co. sewn in a silver stitch inside
blazer pocket.

Still under spell of some blocky letters
scrawled in a quick hand, a sign taped
to soda machine spelled out: OUT OF ORDER.
How it turned out is the wrong thing
        to ask. Turn in your badge:
OK, another bit job in the dust, the local
        pharmacy shrink-wrapped pallet.
The spider plant was a horror, yet what do you do
if you're a cascading horror? Be a filter, or
        own your own ugly.
Your best and worst days were a book,
yet late in the game one friend appeared
        from the thin air.
His basement full of Verve Records in milk crates.

September and March are beginning again.
So drop the script for your screenplay and release
        your hands, a long pause here.
One good voice in your head;
            living off the air,
400 No Shows. When everything else is spent—
throw your body there. Down by law
        and all your drowned-out calls.
Throw your body at the mark again. *It's dangerous*
to close your eyes
for too long, quoth the brute image.
Not an intersection, but a series of circles
        and towns that continue
to roll through everything—the nearby noise
        of a fight song, a wild marching band of memory.
By late morning the traffic is thinning to a tilt though soon
will be monstrous again. Think tea, drink coffee.
The light's green: take the side road out.

groundwork

The Pre-History of March

Don't say scrapes, or nylon stitches
Say blood and the light in a glass of water
Say you're playing a game of wireball with gravity
Say you're not keeping score, but falling behind
Say ready or not
Say the lack of eye contact, or not even looking
Say he's slow, the turtle, little shit, *you're it*
Say this line is blank
Say it will take years
Say it will take longer than that
Say the day and night will be your witness
Say you will be your own proof
Say it's the time before the time to sleep
Say the dream can be wakeful
Say the days are not done, though some will be dusted
Say the cold will still be cold
Say the words *all* and *together* together
Say if no contact now, then a rendezvous
Say the hard bones have yet to be born
Say that somewhere there is a room
Say you are in that room right now

Darkroom Diaries

Diary found in a darkroom at Moore College of Art
dated 1972

Tuesday September 19th
The fresh air will kill you.

Tuesday Sept 26th
The radio in the next room tuned to a classical music station
all night.

Tuesday Oct 2nd
Eskimo headgear in the Museum.

At Shelley's drugstore kids rode up on their bikes and handlebars.

Tuesday Oct 9th
Fell asleep on bed while smoking, woke up to smoke everywhere,
ran outside with the smoldering navy comforter.

Tuesday Oct 16th
A piece of scrap paper found in my pocket: "But there is still time
to save the lives of your children" written in pencil.

Tuesday
My legs are dolphins that cut across the surf.

Tuesday Nov 2nd
Awake again: sleep, dream, the Andy Williams show, drink.

Some people came in wearing trench coats.

Tuesday Nov 9th
Susan said it's forbidden for our pictures to echo
the objects they depict; nothing looks like that,
she said, but it's allowed, it's allowed
for the world to look the way it does.
Fine words those.

Tues Nov 16th
One more night, still here.

Tuesday Nov 23rd
Some nights you skip.

Tuesday Nov 30th
Cold Sunday afternoon grandmother's block in Orange NJ:
the smooth slate pavements where I roller skated as a kid are all broken
up by the massive roots of the old red oaks. Took many photographs.
The many sides of the sidewalk.

Tuesday Dec 6th
The tunnel leads to probably the deadest area in the city.

Sonny Rollins
playing "St. Thomas."
We are not found out.
Only Sarah McEneaney's dog Trixie and me
dancing Calypso.
The rhythm and tune, Trixie's large bright eyes.
She's no dummy only a perfect patchwork
of black & white & brown.
Take a solo—upright bass tenor sax & drums.
No that's not a real solo—that's the bass, high hat
& Trixie—Saint Trixie herself!

Tuesday Dec 13th
Prints are not reproductions. Susan said this is a mistaken idea.
What you're looking at is a photograph: how something looks there.

After class Lara said: "There are many good reasons not to quote Julius
Caesar. That is all I will say," she said.

*

Undated Entries:

Glamour: a starlet in an Alpine ski town.

It doesn't just happen in novels; it doesn't just happen in the movies.
"It's theater for somebody, somewhere." And *It* loved to happen in
every diary I've ever read. Like Marcus Aurelius always said:
Be not too eager. Thanks for the book Dad!

*

bodies. thresholds.
Two or three hundred color snapshots on the bathroom wall.
Flawless Sabrina through the door—
"No saints in three acts," she declares.

On your mark, get set, pull back—
Jack D's electrical tape face-lift.

Two more Moore Menthols for the tall lady in the living room,
the top few buttons of her purple dress open, her hairy chest, beautiful.
She's been getting a blow job for the past five mins. [stet, text with
strikethrough]

DD (who took me here to meet Jack) was checking around on the plants;
now he's at the fireplace making (and partly burning) Jiffy Pop
          buttered popcorn as it erupts through the tinfoil—

                    *

Peter Hujar's reclining portrait of May Wilson: a photographic
Matisse—the color of the arabesque only richer in the silver print.

                         I want to love in that world.

                    *

From the time I was twelve I wanted to marry Van Morrison.
What a jerk.

                    *

Avedon and Baldwin's disturbing and gorgeous *Nothing Personal*.
(The black glossiness of the black borders). That we are all custodians
of something more—every face an argument against cultural suicide,
and suicide itself.

                    *

Vinegar, Mayo, Hardboiled Eggs. No Thanks.

                    *

A picture postcard from Ingrid:

Her light sailboat penmanship on the back.
Steel Pier Atlantic City in soft watercolors on the front.
The watercolors are the color of saltwater taffy.
Someone said that they made up all those flavors down there,
but it's a lie, a beautiful lie.

Pete Rose Meet Zoe Strauss

There are people who can teach you

how to swim, and eventually, how to dive.

But diving into home plate is a whole other thing.

How fright and light are the self-same sparks. Who said that? I did.

Pete Rose taught us kids how baseball was played. Now hit the dirt.

When I gave Zoe my two Pete Rose books, she

grabbed my arms and jumped up and down—

she went off like the Lottery.

The 1980 Phillies *racing* to the pitcher's mound to pile on

in *a dance-around-circle* around Tug McGraw.

You want to talk Pete Rose, Zoe said. They called me Ms. Charlie Hustle.

Honest to God, it's engraved on my 5th grade softball trophy right there:

MS. CHARLIE HUSTLE

Heads Up

I'm keeping my eye on a hawk flying
over 21st and Market.
For all I know the hawk is keeping an eye on me.
        Yesterday the Federal Reserve Bank escaped
being hacked because of a spelling error.
And more events,   but my head is here.
For the moment I can breathe in blue, breathe in green,
breathe out gold.
        A billboard-sized kid running bold in a Blue Cross ad,
baseball glove   reaching into the sky "Live Fearlessly."
Trouble afoot and above, you name it. The hawk and me
keeping an eye on that ball and to see who will have
first dibs on the kid.

Private Far-Off Places

The greatest love poems in the world have nothing to do
     with it.
A man's face, quiet, and skinny-cool body
     in an Italian foreign language class.
The force of a dear woman's mind and body melded
     in a lemon-colored dress.
Not a flash in the pan, though that too fills a peripheral need.
It's the impeccable tempo of our French friend's questions
opening up to more one-at-a-time questions
     and perfectly timed pauses, taking us
to private far-off places—to here and here again, all new.
The calm, late-night focus of your companionship.
Assured in words not to be reassured in words.
No promises past the page only all the moment can hold.
As fast and as slow and as stunning as an eclipse.
Given over to this given moment,
worthy of a Nobel in Ethics, attending to our attentions.
The weight of a good fork, the small joys of a good lunch,
     and lunch itself.
Talk-singing the lyrics of "I Got a Gal in Kalamazoo."
The quality of a line related to the next. Again
     and again, I fall,
a ballet of attendant parts falling: the good, the bad,
     and the lovely, *a counterpart of what we are.*
Enough for the night, early morning, and a lonesome
     afternoon.
Here before the crumbs of the morning toast can be wiped
from the table.
In "If the Birds Knew" I remember you said:
   "Not only as though the danger did not exist
But as though the birds were in on the secret."

Today the sweltering heat has passed and the wind is soft
        and cool.
Today the wind is not so windy, a perfect morning really.
Not the wind that hit me from all sides, in the back of a JEEP
        to Atlantic City a few weeks earlier.
At 75 mps light rain isn't so light.
The unruly wind, straight from central casting,
is our dumb dumb guru, constant friend, diligent teacher.
Drying me off as quickly as the clouds cross the highway.
No, we never pull over to put up the top.
The back-and-forth play of wind and rain: wet hair,
        dry hair, wet air, dry air.
It's not only glorious dogs who appreciate the charms
        of the wind.
Cup my hands over my ears, let go. Cup. Let go.
Sometimes hold my hand out the side window like a child.
Surf the powerful air—do it again.
When my friends glance back, break my pose,
        and make more faces. People driving by look twice.
I laugh out loud, as loud as I can, loud as a runway.
I breathe in. I realize I am someone else. I was somewhere else.
E was in the doorway and proudly translating for the cats,
explaining: "It wasn't bad of Rupert to wake us up last night.
The kitties said, *No no no—come here, I have something to tell you.*
That mouse was in our house—The House Mouse.
Ru wanted to tell us he did something good for us;
for over thousands of years he was bred to do it!"
Delight in the dark, the well-told tale of last night's caper.
Old windy rumors of instinct and love, a beautiful dead mouse
between us, and for the moment, its soft gray fur licked clean.

The 1,000-Year Storm

The basement wall is not a wall
Only stones soaked through.
Sheets of rain and sheets and blankets,
Your eyes softer and softer.
Water streams under the faux French doors
      on the basement floor.
A $1,000 deductible—
      for the 1,000-year storm.
All reports arranged to float or sink,
Cars not stuck near Gladwyne, float
At Conshohocken; on Midvale
Floodwater sweeps woman under;
The sound of water, a truck parked nearby.
Double-crossed at Trenton, boats
      are ordered to moor;
Washington's Reenactors revolt.
Not a drizzle nor merely a downpour—
It is *that* kind of rain.
Hold the space, take their place,
Clouds replace the clouds.

Groundwork

Wet cement has a remote voice
      and concrete none.
Inside, I am inside my head. Outside are the men.
A sledgehammer in the air, men thinking,
working.
Sparks fly from
      the men's dusty mouths,
their chalk lines and wisecracking,
      and all the high heavens between.
Out the back storm door, I don't know enough
not to listen, or hear their cursing.
A man from the neighborhood says there had easily
been three feet of concrete poured into that patio
years before.

Up overhead the hammer part of the sledgehammer
                  lighter than air
and its deep thud down.

A long pause, and a heavy thud again.

Children on job sites draw so many maps.
A dozen men will take this one with them.
Seven men are convinced it can be done—
      they'll wear another face
          when they get one.
              They work the slab
from every side, turn every inch.
In the yard the cement may never end, but it must.

Poem

Today, the first of the year, I write
in concern for my father.
His busted knees, a whole body ache.
His face says more than he does when he says
"I feel better now."

Today, take a walk. Today, call your father.
Sweep the floor.

Shower and wash hair.
Don't turn on TV or go online.
Out my window the vibrations tell me
that two buildings are going up fast.

Today start later, and again. The book
I've been calling *Tell A Story*, or
This is What I Heard. But how to do it, or
say? soaked in and out, all but a watermark.

Today, Jan. 5th, find myself as clear
in my heart as I've ever been, and this too
shall pass.   And say to no one
that I do not mind saying 'I' because
I know that the universe is connected
and this is my portion.

Today, if I knew my own vanity
exactly how would I tell it? A hidden hand
already tipped?

Today, the thinnest bunch of winter branches join
in a swath of pencil-thin plumes.

Keep starting off but getting no nearer to age twelve.
Can't remember a thing, though there are days
I know it wasn't me at all.

Pant leg ripped across the back of the leg,
more close calls too much sun;
scale   a fence, move along the side of the building
the rooftop, and another curve of a corner.
The soft silver and tar-blackened roof space.
And those pitched black, black windows boxes—
stopping everywhere, beginning
nowhere.

Hungry, again.
I was always hungry.

Near noon, shake it off.
Finally cold, finally January and the year,
if only now   here as much as I ever was.
New enough for something new,
a song, a season—
ice in the river-colored lead,
a pencil number 2.

Today, I write right pass that kid,
the one who I asked to tell me,
        the way he looked right at me:
scar on the chin, and the burn smacked right
across his face.

Concentrate and Continue

There, where the first and last gods kept their tents.

There, where your jaw released a smile.

There, where the good guys didn't win and were not guys.

There, where the page was torn and the morning song continued, nearly unnoticed.

There, where another door would be open to arms reaching for arms that were reaching for them.

There, where the floor did sing, no need to run love aground, the floor did sing.

There, where on getting home from the dance you shut the door and danced each step exactly as it was, curtain to curtain.

There, where you were finally released from the dance.

There, where you had no wallet but twenty-three singles and some looser change.

There, where in the molecular air, you let the construction sounds wash over you.

There, where *lost sight* walked away from the perpetual pointing of the seeing world.

There, where there would be no need to say something untrue.

There, where your wildest thoughts alighted and you escaped through a pinhole.

Not to hear the music, but to have felt song

Whatever the day, or day before that, the feeling
was of sun and grandfather sitting.   Working
my way around the narrow side of the duplex's
back-yard. The rhubarb's plumes as tall as me and
the chain-link fence.   And later at the fish hatcheries,
for hours more on end, a crooked concrete chain
of shallow concrete pools, which I can hear.
The warmth on my neck, and no pressure at all.
You and the folding chair were simply there.

Look Me in the Face Sonnet

A side effect of the side effects and a bone-cold day.
The aunt who was more than an aunt came closer
And asked, You alright? Well that's not you.
Not the guy I know. Stop fretting, let's talk. Nobody else
Can tell your story. WHO has that? And me, she said,
What do I want? Look me in the face. OK. I do and
Sit and find out she's been sick for six months.
Why tell? she said. Anyway I'm telling you now:
My body hurts like hell, but my brain is fine.
My appetite is amazing. I'M STILL ME. Do me a favor
And sit for another minute, we don't have to talk so much.
You're hooked with the phone and *the everything else.*
Unplug. Leave it HOME, wherever that is.
When you're doing the dishes: DO the dishes. Tunneling?
Dig the tunnel. Telling a story, tell it to ME.
There's no secret to what we need.

from **Things We String Together**

Familiar as a weeknight and as maddening.

You keep on your way, your erratic way,
        hungrily, figured by you
and your relationship to God: Sister.
It's not true you will never tell
what you know—

I couldn't explain it to anyone.

Aware of a snag
        of fiber on your hand. You stop,
keep the edge,
        the last click for now.

One striped orange handbag full of beads, so many
shoelaces, a hatchery, those clicking beads.
                Colorful hoard—
your private stash and treasure.

Pointing in the doorway,

        your face, hurt then.

"No, no, there's nothing out there."

You only want what you want and there is no reason
not to pitch a fit.

        Before you stormed off
I wanted you to look at me.
Before I stormed off, thoughts rankled me—

When it comes to being furious maybe we're even.

Your face is kind of tough:
fair, defiant, half hidden in your name.

You look Irish. A bit of South Orange, that
        North Jersey brusque.

        Heart of amber, heart of spunk.
Do you invent me as much as I invent you?
I know we can lock in. I know we can again.

We cannot know each other.
But we have a thread,
        share the humid September heat.
God comes to see us without a bell.
                From a sudden hunger you step away,
jangle, follow your nose,
                your breath, our hardheaded heads.

You've had a few jobs. My favorite,
        unwrapping bubble gum that never sold.
Each day they'd cart away the old chewing gum,
then
        mix it all up again like new.
Did you cut into the profits? Are you chewing
some right now?

When you dance you don't want to dance with anyone else, except
maybe Tommy Bandford or Gina Coccia, just not with me.

Sometimes you kick your feet, sometimes
        you spin, just once.

Your main move is leg-to-leg.
You get going,
        it's remarkable. You plant your feet,
they don't move at all: you sway.

When you clap your hands you laugh.

You peel off. Done.

By now I think I'd know what you are going to do, but don't.

But you're predictable as anyone.

You'd rather stay in. You'd rather not swim. Bowling is for suckers,
        but fun to hang out.

Sometimes you fake tears. And so? So I know. And so?

We are stubborn.
        We resent showing our hand.
We can't help but to show them.

I won't call these bricks and things "toys."

Another bag:
        you hold the string beads and shake.
It's not manic, not voodoo, not superstitious.

All sorts of clicks, or is it only one
click: wood
        block
on wood

Wood that listens.

                *

You know exactly what you like, Bold Bean,
and where to find it:
seven dollars plus tax is joy at a steal.
Stock up on clear blue containers and a variety of electrical tape.
Scissors and reversible tape—you have a mission.
Plastic party Dollar Store everything in your bag.

Back home, on the job
          of broken plastic bits.

Always working, enlisting others—

Looking hard at, searching through your stuff,

Identifying wads of red, black, and impossible-to-rip gray
          tape that has already been taped, taped-over at least twice.

          *

You watch me, make
          side-eyed contact,
tell me what you want—
               know that I know.
Younger, I must have known before I knew.
You stayed young as I grew.

I know about your long-term crush on K.

I know a hamper of clean socks and clean sweatpants is God.

Out from the laundry room: clean towels for under the sink.
Pointing till I answer: "Yes, yes, your clothes, your beautiful red pajamas"
—and they are.

"Go upstairs. I'll be up in a minute."

You piss me off and I piss you off—
                              your junk spilled
                                        all down the stairs.

                    *

When I've been away, you remember
after dinner to tug my hand for bed.

You hand me a clean pillowcase, I hand it right back
to put it on yourself.

I shake out your quilt, waving it over your laughter
—you'll push me away.

Later you check to see if everyone's home.

                    *

I wonder where you think I am when I'm not here, or
how much you think of me at all.

Your footsteps through the sleeping house, putting every thing
in its place,
                    or a place you find.
The next day's search
for your night's work: wallets, shoes, stack of bills,
all moved elsewhere.

                    *

Mom, Grandmom, and Aunt Sharon all have dreams where
you talk to them.
I too look for your language—though
I fear what you'd probably say

we wouldn't want to hear—
As I say nothing here of sex or all the words
we've put in your mouth—

To me you say nothing and I write it down as fast as I can.

1998/2014

The Last Topiary

Once in a row house garden there grew a shrub.
A bold afternoon light fell in love with the shrub.
They were highly similar: the Shrub—trim and shiny,
and the Light—generous and flattering as a postcard.
Years went by. The Light and the Shrub
had folded back away from the street
in front of them. The world was going to hell.
The world had gone to hell, but they were old friends
and they'd keep on doing what they had always done.

Notes

Getting to Philadelphia is a selection of my Philadelphia related poems. There is a geography stretching out in radiating circles beyond the scope of the city or any mapping software.

Sincere thanks to Bob Hershon, Caroline Hagood, and Marie Carter at Hanging Loose Press. I am a lifelong fan of the press and I am honored to publish this collection with them. Heartfelt thanks to Jay Kirk, Cynthia Arrieu-King, L.S. Asekoff, Amy Sadao, and Eleanor Wilner. The book is dedicated to Fran Ryan, labor historian and poet.

Zoe Strauss is a photographer and activist. Her intimate photograph on the Frank El train was taken in high school. It is included here on page ##. Several poems in the collection are in conversation with Zoe's photographs, or dedicated to her, which include: "OREGON AVE," "Pete Rose Poem," and "The Blue Stoop."

The correct spelling of Steve, Tommy, and Michael Flis's last name is Flis – not *Fliss*, which is how it is pronounced, and as it appears in "The Blue Stoop."

In 2014 my book *The Picture that Remains* was published by the Philadelphia Print Center with photographs by Will Brown. In Brown's photographs from the 70s, layers of the city are visible all at once, and often, all in one block. Brown's photograph appears on page ##.

I am grateful to Leroy Johnson for permission to use his painting for the cover art. I am a longtime fan of Johnson and his mixed media inner city Philadelphia landscapes.

Great thanks to photo curator Peter Barberie. He invited me to write poems (including "Darkroom Diaries") about his show *Common Ground: Eight Philadelphia Photographers in the 1960s and 1970s* at the Philadelphia Museum of Art. Peter introduced me to Will Brown. Peter also introduced me to the Ivorian photographer Ananias Léki Dago. Dago's photograph is on the back cover of this book. The photo is a vision. Peter was the curator of the landmark *Zoe Strauss: Ten Years* at the P.M.A.

The 1997 Macy's Thanksgiving Day Parade mentioned in my poem "Getting to Philadelphia" is one of the most infamous Thanksgiving Day parades to date. Many people were hurt or injured and over a dozen iconic balloons were either damaged or destroyed by the wind.

In "The Legend of Cornbread," I directly borrow a construction: "*don't cross 24th Street because…*" from Jefferey McDaniel's poem "Origins" published in his riveting 2008 collection *The Endarkenment*.

My poem "Brilliant Corners" is a map of a life fortified by music. From my early teens to my late 20s I was a musician and started off college as a music major. The poem is dedicated to the visual artist Jennie C. Jones. At parties Jones and I often wind up in a corner somewhere talking up a storm about our appetites for sound. It dawned on me that Thelonious Monk's "Brilliant Corners" is an apt description of some of Jennie's work. Now I realize that in those passionate, hilarious, extended conversations, Jennie and I were both swapping notes about our own sonic lodestars.

Some dedications include: "Sessler's or Hibberd's Bookstore?" for Bob Hershon, "River Song" for Meg Baird, "Morning in Runnemede" and "Private Far-Off Places" for John Ashbery, "Look Me in the Face Sonnet" for Marilyn Kane, "Things We String Together," for my sister Colleen.

I wish to acknowledge my high school English teacher Louis McKee. Lou was a poet and an editor of *The Painted Bride Quarterly*. Lou was a mentor and a friend. Some of the poets Lou first recommended were Lamont Steptoe, Eleanor Wilner, Sonia Sanchez, Tim Dlugos, and Joseph Banford. Here is Lou's lyric "A City Education."

A City Education

> We didn't learn that stuff
> growing up in the city:
> trees were trees, and birds
> except for pigeons and gulls,
> were birds. That is how
> city kids get their attitudes,
> the audacity to suppose
> they can see things
> their own way, do as they like.
> When we were kids in the city

we knew our neighborhoods,
we named the trees and birds
ourselves. They answered us.

Index

From *The Picture that Remains* | 2014 | photographs by Will Brown | The Print Center

> A Week in the Childhood of W.C. Fields
> Mr. Uska and his Dog
> That Old Block
> Saturday Night Special
> The Best Styles
> Don Cook's Brother's Cadillac
> Rear Window
> Algon Avenue
> The Picture that Remains
> The Last Topiary

From *A Series of Small Boxes* | 2007 | Fish Drum

> Trying to live as if it were morning
> Deliberate: Ode for Lorenzo Thomas
> Private Far-Off Places
> The 1,000-Year Storm

From *The American Pragmatist Fell in Love* | 1999 | Banshee Press

> Getting to Philadelphia
> They're fighting in Atlantic City, in Atlantic City